60 Meditations
for a Mindful Life

OTHER NEWT LIST BOOKS
BY ERNEST HOLMES

Creative Mind

Creative Mind and Success

Ernest Holmes Speaks

How to Use Your Power:
20 Practical Lessons for Creating A Balanced Life

Life Is What You Make It

60 Meditations for a Mindful Life

The Basics of Spiritual Mind Healing

The Bible in Light of Spiritual Philosophy

The Meaning of the Bible

The Philosophy of Emerson

The Power of This Thing Called Life

60 Meditations

for a

Mindful life

Updated and Gender-Neutral

Ernest Holmes

newt
LIST

A Newt List Publication

Chicago • New York

Contents

Contents

Foreword

The reader is about to enter into an experience of the words of Ernest Holmes. Any who are aware of the twentieth century author, spiritual leader, and progenitor of The Science of Mind philosophy will recognize the uplift, the crispness, and the clarity of his words. In my readings of his works, I recognized that there is not a single morbid word anywhere in the body of his writings. His is the effort of one whose belief in the Infinite was strong, active, and vibrant.

These meditations handle all subjects of interest to the reader, so all will find something of interest and value. But even if we are not looking in a particular vein of interest, we cannot fail to be uplifted by the simple beauty of Holmes' contributions.

The reader will notice that all the sentences are couched in the first person so that each person can take all the words to heart and know that they have deep, personal meaning. There is such power in Holmes' words: "I live because life lives in me. I believe that all mistakes I ever made are swallowed up in a love, a peace, and a life greater than I am." We can feel the depth of inspiration filling us as we read these meditations or perhaps even speak them aloud.

As readers, we are taking a wonderful spiritual journey as we travel through Ernest Holmes' thoughts through these meditations. For us, the way is clear, the winds calm and comforting, and the destination surely one of spiritual completion.

—*Dr. Margaret Stortz*
Author of Essays on Everything

Introduction

Whether you call the meditations in this book *prayers* or *affirmations* or *treatments*, each one was designed specifically for you. Though they were written a long time ago, each time you read one you make it personal to yourself, because each meditation announces the truth about you, where you are in your life right now.

These meditations are not wishes or statements of hope—what you want to be at some future point in your life or what you hope will one day be true about you. They affirm who you are right now as a member of the human race, as a mindful, spiritual person living in a world peopled with other mindful, spiritual people. They are the truth about each one of us, because we are all derived from the same source and have our true existence as one with that source.

Words are only words until we know they are true, and then they become transformative. So when you read these meditations, whether you select them randomly or in sequence, whether you read one a day or several, it is good to believe—to know—that they are authentically true for you as you speak them. Even if they do not mirror the temporary circumstances you find yourself in, you can be sure that they are the reality about you because they reflect the reality of life, how it works, and your place in it.

To be most effective, prayer should be active. Use the provided "My Meditation" pages to personalize the meditation for you. Record your thoughts here about what you've just read. Draw pictures if that's how you feel. Use this page to inspire the prayer to speak directly to your experience.

Written by Ernest Holmes for his radio program "This Thing Called Life," which aired from the late 1940 through the 1950s, the meditations in this book were heard over the years by thousands who, in hearing them, were changed in the way they thought about themselves, and accordingly changed their lives by embodying the truth they gave. Now, they will do the same for you.

One with God

There is a key to right living. That key is prayer, affirmative prayer. Prayer is our direct line of communion with God. Through affirmative prayer, we learn to clear our minds of negative thoughts, of doubt and fear. This we must do if we are to become aware of the presence of God within and around us.

Take this as your prayer for today: "Do you not know that you are the temple of the living God?" Affirming God's presence here and now, shut every other thought out of your mind, all the distractions of the moment—the doorbell, the telephone—as you listen confidently, peacefully, quietly.

I live because life lives in me. I move because there is a universal energy activating me. I think because there is a universal mind thinking through me. I exist because the Spirit has seen fit to give me life. God never makes mistakes. This is why I am the temple of the living God. There is a divine spark in everyone.

Knowing that I am one with God, and recognizing that all people live and move and have their being in that one Spirit which is God, I know that I am one with every person I meet. Knowing that love must be at the root of all reality, I feel a deep affection for everyone I meet. Forgiving myself for all mistakes I have ever made, and forgiving all others, I seem to meet people in the simplicity of faith, in the harmony of peace, and in the joy of living.

I sincerely believe that there is a divine presence and a law of good that attracts every person and every thing to me, a presence that belongs to me and that, flowing through me, reaches out to everything in my life with love, with consideration, in joy and gladness.

I am learning to salute God in everyone. I meet people naturally, spontaneously, and happily. It is my desire that everyone I meet will be blessed, will feel the warmth and color and friendship that I have for the whole world. I rest in this blessed assurance that we are all one in God.

My Meditation

Abundance

There is a key to right living, a golden key to happiness and success. This key is affirmative prayer, because prayer is our direct line of communion with God. It is through this communion that we clear the mind of negative thoughts, of doubts and fears. This we must do if we are to become aware of the presence of God within and around us.

Use this meditation in affirming God's bounty. Shut every other thought out of your mind so that there will be nothing to disturb you in this moment of your acceptance as you enter into your meditation confidently, joyfully, and quietly.

I now acknowledge God, the divine Spirit, as a living presence in everything and in everyone. I bless everyone I meet. I praise everything I do. I acknowledge God's abundance, the outpouring of the Spirit, the manifestation of life everywhere. I bless my family. I praise my friends. I rejoice in the activities of my life.

I know that love does not condemn and life does not destroy. I sincerely desire that every thought of my mind and every impulse of my whole being will be constructive and life-giving and will radiate that which I now believe and accept to be at the center of my being—the light that lights everyone's pathway.

I bless the small things in my life, that they may multiply and become great. I bless everything that seems little, that it will increase. I bless that which is good, and I desire that good alone will reach out from me to meet the need in everyone, in love, in joy, and with thanksgiving.

MEDITATIONS

My Meditation

You Are Always with Me

There is a golden key to right living. That key is prayer, affirmative prayer. Prayer is our direct line of communion with God. Through affirmative prayer, we learn to clear our minds of negative thoughts, of doubt and fear. This we must do if we are to become aware of the presence of God within and around us.

Take this thought as your prayer for today: "You are always with me, and all that I have is yours." Affirm God's presence here and now as you shut every other thought out of the mind and listen, confidently, peacefully, and quietly.

Realizing that you are in an ever-present good, and, believing that this law of good can bring everything that is desirable into your experience, begin to think and act as though every wrong condition of yesterday were being converted into something new and better. Consciously try to feel that there is nothing in the universe that holds anything against you, and that there is nothing in you that has any resentment against any person or any condition or any thing.

I believe that all the mistakes I ever made are swallowed up in a love, a peace, and a life greater than I am. I surrender all my past mistakes into the keeping of this ever-present, divine, and perfect life.

I feel that love is guiding me into kindness and cooperation with life, into a real, deep, and sincere affection for everyone. I turn my whole thought to the belief that today is a fresh beginning, a new start, a joyous adventure on the pathway of an eternal progress. I am trusting love to guide me. I believe that love guides everyone. I am learning to see the good in everyone and to rejoice in it.

I feel that today is bright with hope and happy with fulfillment. I know that tonight I will sleep in peace. I will awake in joy. I live in the sure knowledge that good alone governs.

My Meditation

Unlimited Supply

If there is a problem of supply in your life, you can solve it through using the same law that Jesus used, and in the same way. Let us follow his teaching and begin this moment to demonstrate abundance.

I live and move and have my being in the eternal presence of God. I realize that this is the unlimited source of all supply. I know that divine intelligence knows how to create its own channels of expression, and, even in ways I know not of, my good comes to me.

I state my need and enfold it in thoughts of abundance. The principle of increase manifests itself through me to meet my every need of my immediate experience. I am an abundant person. I think and feel abundance. I live in a constant expectancy of an ever greater good.

There is nothing in my mind that denies rejects or limits the flow of divine substance into and through my experience. There is only acceptance of God's presence and the divine law of increase.

Infinite intelligence now inwardly instructs me as to the wise use of all the good I have. There is that within me which lovingly shares and expresses the abundance that I have and the abundance that I am. I thank you, Creator, that you have heard, and that you always hear, and that the unlimited measure of your spiritual gifts is set in my heart.

My Meditation

All Things New

There is a power that exists at the very center of your being. You can use that power through affirmative prayer. Prayer is our direct line of communion with God. Through affirmative prayer, we learn to clear our minds of negative thoughts, of doubt and fear. This we must do if we are to become aware of the presence of God within and around us.

As you drop everything else out of the mind, bring in this new day with this thought: "Behold, I make all things new."

I now surrender every doubt and fear, every thought of confusion or uncertainty, into the keeping of the divine Spirit. I loose all sense of limitation, lack, and want into the divine abundance. I lift up the bowl of my acceptance and know that it is filled from the wholeness of plenty. I let God, the supreme intelligence, guide and direct me.

I know that my body is renewed, revitalized, remade. All the energy, action, and vitality in the universe is pouring through me, and I know that every action, every organ and function of this body is created in the wisdom of God and maintained by the power of God.

I look confidently into the future. I see new friendships, new opportunities. Everything in my experience is renewed. Everything is made glad and happy and whole. Now, as I turn to the world around me, I see this same good evenly distributed everywhere and operating through all people.

My Meditation

Your Light

"Let your light so shine before all people, that they may see your good works and glorify your Creator which is in heaven."

In this passage, Jesus is referring to the light that is at the center of your being when he says, "Let your light so shine." Everyone has this light. It comes from our Creator in heaven, who is within each one of us. In prayer and meditation, become aware of this light and truly let it shine. Be very simple but direct about this, completely believing that there is a light at the center of your being and that you are one with all the life there is.

Believing that there is a light which lights everyone's path, and being deeply convinced that this light is also at the center of my own being, I now affirm and accept that there is a power of good at my disposal and that I am immediately one with this power and all of its resources.

I now affirm that divine intelligence guides me, and that I know what to do under every circumstance, that everything in my life is adjusted to harmony, to peace, and to goodness. I know that every idea will come to me that is necessary for complete success. I feel the presence of God as divine companionship, closer to me than my very breath.

I know that the power of good is with me always, and with everyone else, and as I think of others, I am thinking of them as also being guided and directed, loved and guarded into right action, into joy, into peace and happiness, and into success.

My Meditation

Divine Guidance

Feeling that you are one with the divine presence, now seek to enter into conscious communion with it, because this is affirmative prayer and this is spiritual meditation. It is through spiritual meditation that we reach out—or into—the divine presence that fills all space and also finds its dwelling place in the sanctuary of our own heart.

Believing that God is everywhere, and knowing that the divine life can restore my soul, I now affirm and deeply accept divine guidance. I believe that I am sustained by an infinite power, guided by an infinite intelligence, and guarded by an infinite love. I feel this presence in, around, and through me, and through all people.

I am being directed. There is a power greater than I am on which I may rely. I am relying on this power, and I am letting this intelligence govern and guide. I am fully aware of divine love and protection.

My mind is accepting this as the great truth in my life. I lay aside every doubt or fear and enter gladly into a newness of life. I do believe that the Lord is my shepherd. I do believe that the Lord restores my soul.

MEDITATIONS

My Meditation

An Answer

"You shall call on the Lord, and the Lord will answer."

There is a power for good in the universe available to all of us. Our approach to this power is through faith, prayer, and conviction, because faith and prayer are our communion with the invisible, with This Thing Called Life. It is through communion that we make our requests known and through faith that we receive an answer.

Shut every other thought from the mind, everything that could distract your attention, and listen quietly and peacefully, but with deep and sincere trust.

I do believe that the law of good is around me. I do believe that divine love, acting through this law, can and will meet all my needs. I am entering into the peace and quiet of this thought with absolute conviction as I affirm that in the divine presence there is fullness of life for me and for everyone I may be thinking of.

I accept divine guidance in everything I do. I believe a power greater than I am will bring to me this day the love, the happiness, and the friendship that I wish for the whole world. I believe that today I will have the opportunity to comfort and help everyone I meet, and, in so doing, I know that I will be blessed with the joy of giving as well as the happiness of receiving.

I expect to be happy. I anticipate goodness. I enter into peace. I know that as I "call on the Lord" and the law of good, I will receive a direct answer. May this good I am to receive become a blessing to everyone I meet.

My Meditation

Perfect Body

"The spirit of God has made me, and the breath of the Almighty has given me life."

Through prayer and meditation, we connect our thought with the Spirit that has created us and our physical bodies with the breath of all life. There is one divine and perfect life in which we all live, move, and have our being. We wish to draw close to this life and breathe its Spirit into our own being. Do this quietly, reverently, and with a sense of complete acceptance.

My body is the temple of the living God, and I believe in the ability and the willingness of Spirit to sustain its own creation. I believe that every organ and function of my physical body is animated by the living Spirit within me. I have complete confidence in this Spirit. I know that I am loved of this Spirit and needed by it. I feel at home with it.

There is no condemnation, no judgment, and no fear in me. I feel that I belong to the world in which I live, that I love people and am loved by them. I have a deep sense of confidence and trust. I feel that I am secure in life and that I need no longer be anxious about anything. I am laying all my fears and doubts aside and entering into quiet communion with the Spirit of confidence, of faith, and of acceptance.

I feel that my whole being is renewed, invigorated, and made alive. There is complete stillness and perfect peace at the center of my being as I wait on the presence that makes all things perfect.

MEDITATIONS

My Meditation

The Power

"*To as many as believed, gave God the power.*"

We are one with the divine power, and it is now meeting all our needs. As you quietly turn to this presence, put all other thoughts out of the mind as you listen deeply, joyously, and expectantly.

I believe in the power greater than I am. I believe in the divine presence in which I live and move and have my being. I am thinking back to the center of my being, where this presence exists in all its beauty and all its peace.

I know that divine intelligence helps me to control my thinking and causes me to live with joy and in calm expectancy of good. I am permitting myself to be guided by this intelligence. As I wait on it and let it flow through me and out into action, I know that I will be guided in everything I do. I know I will bless everyone I meet. I will bring new life to every situation I contact.

My whole mind and thought responds with complete conviction, and I feel that today and every day the power of the living Spirit flows through me and makes perfect the way before me, radiating joy and love to everyone and to everything.

My Meditation

The Seed of Good

"The seed is the word of God."

Meditation does two things for us: one, we might call passive; the other, active. Passive means that meditation helps us to recognize the divine presence and feel it deep within our own being, and then helps us to realize that the Spirit within us is at one with the Spirit of God. The active part of meditation is where we use the law of good for definite purposes, because we are all surrounded by a creative mind that responds to our belief in it.

Realize that your faith acts as a seed planted in the creative soil. You do the planting, but God gives you the harvest.

Believing that my word is the seed of good, and that the divine giver of all life wills me to have a harvest, I plant this seed in the warm, rich soil of divine love and bury it in my faith. I know that from this seed, which is my word, and from that power of good greater than I am, which is the law of God, I will receive a harvest.

This is the springtime of my hope, and I desire that love, peace, and confidence will envelop me and everyone I meet as I sit in the garden of God, my Garden of Eden. I desire that joy and happiness will go forth from me to make glad the life of every other person as I wait on the Creator. I am planting seeds of happiness, of friendship, of love, of goodwill for myself, for everyone I know, and for the whole world.

Not alone in my garden do I wish these seeds to grow, but I pray that I may broadcast them wherever I walk, and, uniting with all others in faith, I rest in the supreme assurance that the life the whole world seeks will find fruitage in the garden of love that I am planting today.

MEDITATIONS

My Meditation

Tend Your Garden

Today you are cultivating your garden. You are pulling up the weeds of uncertainty and carefully nurturing your thoughts of faith and confidence in This Thing Called Life, in the power greater than you are, in God, the living Spirit, not some mighty, but all-mighty. Do not be weary in well doing, because in due season you will reap if you faint not. As you carry this simple thought back into your mind, you are lifting up your whole thought to the sunshine and rain from heaven, and you are knowing that a power greater than you are is seeing to it that the seeds of your expectancy are sprouting in the garden of your desire.

I have planted my garden, and I know that the Creator of the harvest will give the increase. As I go about the everyday activities of living, I confidently expect to meet with happiness and with success. I believe that deep within me is the well-spring of eternal life. I believe that around me is the joy of living. I believe that I am sustained by a divine power and guided by an infinite wisdom.

No thought of fear can assail me, no doubt can enter my consciousness, no uncertainty can grow in my garden, because I have planted it in the mind of God. I have planted it with hope, with conviction, and in certainty. I am awaiting the harvest with a song of joy in my heart.

I have not planted this garden for myself alone, but that I may share it with others. I will have plenty to spare, an abundance of love, an excess of goodwill. I have planted tenderness and compassion here so that others may come and eat of the fruits of the garden of life with me. There will be no strangers in my garden, because God's sun and rain come alike to the gardens of every soul. I enter into communion with others as I walk in the garden of life and sit under the shade of the tree of peace and love.

My Meditation

A Solution

Prayer and meditation help us draw closer to the divine presence and enter into conscious communion with it. Prayer and meditation arrive at the highest point of power and possibility, when all doubt and fear are put aside, when we enter into an affirmative acceptance and when we actually believe that God is right where we are. Shut everything else out of the mind for a few moments as you quietly and confidently affirm the divine presence and come actually to believe that God is guiding you.

"I will lead them in paths that they have not known."

Make this personal to the self as you quietly and confidently enter into conscious communion with the divine Spirit.

I am bringing all my problems to the altar of faith, and I know that every true desire of my heart will be fulfilled through the power of love. My first desire is that all my thoughts and all my acts will give joy and gladness to everyone around me. I wish the healing power of love to flow through me to everyone.

I now believe that divine intelligence, which is the mind of God, is guiding, guarding, and directing my thoughts and acts.

Now, think of some problem in your life that you would like to have solved, and consciously take this problem into your thought, not as a problem, but as though you were receiving the answer.

I believe that God already knows the answer to this problem; therefore, I am letting go of the problem and I am listening to the answer as though it were sure. The answer to this problem not only exists in the mind of God, but I affirm that it is in my mind now, that something in me does know what to do.

I confidently wait on divine good. I expect to be guided. I joyfully accept this guidance with deep gratitude and with a great feeling of love and closeness to the divine presence that I know fills all space. I am open to new ideas, to new thoughts, new hopes and aspirations. That which so recently seemed a problem no longer exists, because the mind of God, which knows the answer, is quietly flowing through my thought and feeling. A great peace and joy come over me as I accept this answer from the giver of all life.

My Meditation

Spiritual Body

Every part of your body is made of spiritual substance. There is a spiritual body that cannot be sick. This body is within you now. It is the mind which blocks the emanation of this spiritual body through the physical form. Jesus knew that there is a spiritual body and a perfect body. Seeing this perfect body instead of a diseased form, he was able to heal every manner of illness.

When you say that your body is spiritual, you are not denying your physical body. The physical is included within the spiritual. If the Spirit has seen fit to express itself through a physical universe and to give you a physical body, it would be absurd to think of your body or environment as an illusion, unworthy of your attention. Rather, you should think of these as things of joy. Every statement you make about your body, or any belief you hold about it that causes the mind to accept Spirit as the substance of your body, tends to heal.

My body is the temple of the living Spirit. It is spiritual substance now. Every part of my body is in harmony with the living Spirit within me. The life of this divine Spirit flows through every atom of my being, vitalizing, invigorating, and renewing every particle of my physical body. There is a pattern of perfection at the center of my being which is now operating through every organ, function, action, and reaction. My body is forever renewed by the Spirit.

I am now made vigorous and whole. I possess the vitality of the Infinite. I am strong and well. The life of the Spirit is my life. All of its strength is my strength. Its power is my power. Every breath I draw is a breath of perfection, vitalizing, building up, and renewing every cell of my body. I am born of the Spirit. I am in the Spirit. I am the Spirit made manifest.

My Meditation

God Is All

"God is over all, in all, and through all."

Believing that there is a divine presence closer to me than my very breath, and realizing that I live in the one perfect Spirit, and knowing that the God around and the God within me is one God, I enter my meditation today.

My Creator, which is in heaven within me, holy is your name. Your realm is come now, and I accept it. I am one with my Creator forever. There is one life, that life is God, that life is my life now, and that life is perfect.

Looking on the circumstances that surround me, I bless them, even as Jesus blessed the bread and broke it. Even as the loaves and fishes multiplied in the outstretched and upturned hand of Jesus' love, so I know that everything in my experience that is good is multiplied and increased.

Even as I feel the increase pressing into my own experience, I give it out with no thought of return, that it may feed and bless others, these others who are some part of me, because God is in them, and God is in me, and we are in each other.

My Meditation

Release the Idea

We are interested in a power greater than we are which we can use. We are interested in divine guidance and how it works. We are interested in prayer and how it is answered. This is called affirmative prayer, the prayer that believes in its own answer. We accept this answer even before we see it. Take as the thought for your meditation today these wonderful words of Jesus: "Whatsoever things you desire, when you pray, believe that you receive them, and you shall have them."

See if you can arrive at an attitude of complete acceptance today. Think of some definite thing you wish to pray for. It doesn't matter what it is, just place it definitely in your mind as an idea.

I am handing this idea over to the divine intelligence, to the power that knows how to do anything. I am handing it over in complete acceptance of its answer. Gratefully and with deep peace, with complete conviction, I am receiving this answer into my experience.

I know there is nothing in me that can doubt either the divine goodness or the operation of its law in my affairs. I believe that everything necessary to the fulfillment of this definite desire is now in full operation, that all the circumstances in my life are tending to bring it about.

If there is anything I ought to do about it, I will receive the impression to act, I will receive guidance, and I will be impelled to act intelligently. Therefore, I have a complete sense of ease and assurance. I look forward joyfully as I anticipate this good that is to come into my life.

I believe that all who are now praying with me will receive the answer to their desires from the same source. My faith goes out to them even as their faith reaches back to me. I believe that out of the great good in which we all live there will surely come to each one of us an answer to our particular need.

My Meditation

Be at Peace

"Acquaint now yourself with God, and be at peace: thereby good shall come unto you."

Through prayer and in meditation, we unify ourselves with the divine presence in everything. We come into closer contact with the living Spirit that is in all things and in all people. There is only one final power and one final presence in all the universe.

As you dwell on the meaning of this passage, see if you cannot more completely enter into union with life. See if you cannot more completely feel that life is flowing out, through, and into your acts, and be certain as you listen quietly and reverently to the Spirit that you are making this meditation personal to yourself.

I know that the divine Spirit is operating through me now. I know that I am not limited by anything that has happened or by anything that is now happening. I am aware that the truth is making me free from any belief in want, lack, or limitation. I have a feeling of security and of ability to do anything that I should do.

I am entering into an entirely new set of conditions and circumstances. That which has no limit is flowing through my consciousness into action. I am guided by the same intelligence and inspired by the same imagination that scatters the moonbeams across the waves and holds the forces of nature in its grasp. I have a calm, inward conviction of my union with good, my oneness with God.

I have complete confidence that the God who is always with me is able and willing to direct everything I do, to control my affairs, to lead me into the pathway of peace and happiness. I free myself from every sense of condemnation, either against myself or others. I lose every sense of animosity. I now understand that there is a principle and a presence in every person, gradually drawing them into the realm of good. I know that the realm of God is at hand, and I am resolved to enter into this realm, to possess it, and to let it possess me.

My Meditation

Spirit Within

The Spirit within me is projecting itself into my experience. Divine intelligence is acting in my affairs. Everything I do, say, or think is governed by this intelligence. The power that creates and sustains everything is now creating everything necessary to my happiness.

It is a law of my life that wherever I go, the path will be prepared before me, made immediate, perfect, plain, straight, and easy. I am compelled to see and understand every opportunity that presents itself and to operate on it intelligently. I am compelled to take any physical action necessary to the manifestation of this word.

There is nothing in me that hinders the Spirit from manifesting itself through me in joy, happiness, and peace. It is the law of my life that wherever I go, I will meet with joy, with love, friendship, gratitude, compensation, and with a complete opportunity for the expression of every talent and ability I possess. Every door is open. Nothing can go forth from me except goodness, truth, love, and kindness, and nothing less than goodness can come back to me.

I identify myself with abundance, health, and happiness. I associate myself with the vast "all-ness." I identify myself with everything necessary to make my life complete. Simply, with complete conviction, I accept my freedom. Letting go of all previous mistakes, I know that I am free and unhindered today. I know that everything I am doing is governed by love and controlled through law. I believe the law of good will bring every good and perfect thing to me and will bless everyone I contact.

My Meditation

Lift Up Your Mind

"If I am lifted up from the earth, I will draw all people to me."

Jesus was talking about the Spirit within him, the person he really was, the one that should be lifted up and exalted. I believe that he was talking about God in you and God in me, as well as God in himself, when he said, "What I have done, you shall do also."

Realize that something greater than you are has given you the power to live, that there must be a place of peace and of wholeness within you. As you meditate on these thoughts, with deep reverence but in complete simplicity, expect a new influx into your life. Expect something wonderful to happen to you.

I am now waiting on the Spirit within me. I believe that I am intimately associated with this Spirit. I believe that I am so close to it that it can reach out through me and govern my life in harmony and in peace. I believe that it can bring joy to me and to everyone I meet. I believe that it can be a blessing to myself and to others.

I am lifting up my whole mind in faith to the conviction that the Spirit of God is within me and that this Spirit is my real self. I am inviting this Spirit to enter my mind, to direct my thoughts and my acts, and I am expecting it to do this.

Believing that I am an individual in God and a divine person in my own right, I am expecting new ideas, new thoughts, new ways of doing things, to stimulate my imagination to action. I am inviting new circumstances and situations into my experience, and I am waiting on the divine presence within me to make itself known, to reveal itself to every person I meet and every situation I contact, to bring life, joy, and happiness to everyone.

My Meditation

The Center

"This is the day the Lord has made; we will rejoice and be glad in it."

Prayer is spiritual communion, and the ideas used in meditation are for the purpose of breaking down the negative thought patterns that deny the good we so greatly need and so earnestly seek. Prayer, spiritual communion, and meditation, to be effective, should be direct, personal, and immediate, so that the words used may become self-realization.

Believing that the Spirit of God is at the center of my own being and at the center of all others, I now invite this divine presence to illumine my thought, to guide me in everything I do.

In this quiet moment of self-realization, I feel that I am meeting this divine presence face to face.

I feel that all the vitality there is, all the energy there is, and all the enthusiasm for life that there is, is flowing through me, circulating through every atom of my physical being, animating every organ, every action, and every function of my physical body with perfect life.

I feel the inflow and the circulation of this Spirit through me, and in joy and gladness I recognize the presence of love and life.

Surely this is the realm of God.

Today, and every day, manna falls from heaven.

This is the day that God has made, and I am glad in it.

My Meditation

The Harvest of Good

"Lift up your eyes and look on the fields; for they are white, already to harvest."

As you look out on your world in your imagination, see the fields of your experience ripe for the harvest. Feel the presence of love, of harmony and of successful living, of joy and friendship. It is through quiet meditation and spiritual affirmation that we actually enter into conscious communion with the divine presence that is always around and within us. Our fields are ready to harvest, so enter into the privilege of communion with your neighbor and with God in the joyful acceptance of the harvest of good that the power greater than you are has created for you.

"The fields are white, already to harvest." As you think about the meaning of these simple but significant words, meditate quietly and with complete acceptance.

I gratefully acknowledge the divine bounty of life. I am thankful for the harvest of good that love has prepared for me. As I gather the fruits of joy and happiness which nature presses back into my hand, I gladly divide them with others.

I expect the garden of my experience to increase in quiet confidence and peace. I keep myself in constant expectation of good, and forever I pray that I may daily have the privilege and the opportunity of extending this good to others. I sincerely desire to be a blessing to everyone I meet. To every situation I contact, I wish to bring joy, hope, and happiness. I dedicate the garden of my soul to the hope that is within me and to the great longing that is in all people.

My Meditation

You Are Not Alone

"Wherefore putting away lying, everyone speak truth with your neighbor, for we are members of one another."

As you pray and meditate, it is good for you to remember that you are not alone. You are part of an ever-growing group of people who believe in a power greater than we are, a power greater than any bomb or other destructive force can be. We believe that this power is a power of good that can be used in human affairs. We believe this power is right where we are and available to us right now, today, and to everyone.

I believe in the union of God with humankind. I believe in the need we all have for each other. I believe that the Spirit is acting through me in love and in harmony with others. I believe that the same Spirit in others is reacting to me in love and in harmony.

I believe that we are all one family in God and that God is working in each one of us in such a way as to produce a better world. I am willing to be guided. I am glad to be led by the Spirit, and I rejoice in the thought that all people live in God, that we all may be guided by the Spirit.

I am seeking and finding love and friendship everywhere I go, in everyone I meet, in every situation in which I find myself.

My Meditation

Family

Believing that God is an actual presence within and around me, and in and around each member of my family, I now affirm that my family is a household of God. Each member is deeply rooted in the one divine spirit of love, of harmony, and of unity. Each desires the good of the other. Here is tolerance, understanding, and peace. Here is a unity of thought, purpose, plan, and action. Here is sympathy and understanding. And here is the joy of living and the happiness of being together.

There is at all times a deep sense of security and safety, a feeling of comfort and well being. There is a feeling that we all belong to each other and that we all belong to life itself. We are in partnership with life and with each other. Joining together in mutual confidence, my family lives and moves and has its being in God. Though each of us are individuals, we unite with all others and are joined together in love. There is always a sense of peace, of protection, and of happiness, because this is God's good family here on earth.

My Meditation

Meditation for Another Person

In your prayer and meditation today, practice drawing closer to the divine presence and more perfectly using that power for good in which we all believe. Dedicate your prayer of affirmation today to someone other than yourself. As you think these thoughts over carefully and prayerfully, seek to feel the divine presence and the divine power in and around the one or ones you are thinking of.

I believe that *[name]* lives and moves and has their being in pure Spirit, in perfect life, in God, the living Spirit. I believe that *[name]* is surrounded by a divine power acting in all of *[name]*'s affairs for good. I believe that perfect life is flowing through *[name]* now. Divine energy is circulating through *[name]*.

[Name] is in rhythm with this life. I believe that every organ, action, and function of *[name]*'s body is in harmony with this divine presence. I believe that all of *[name]*'s affairs are in the keeping of infinite wisdom. I believe that *[name]* is directed and guided so that *[name]* knows what to do under every circumstance.

[Name] is led of the Spirit. I believe that the way is prepared before *[name]*. The doorway of opportunity is open to *[name]*. New friends, new situations, new circumstances present themselves to *[name]*. Always there is a feeling within *[name]* that *[name]* is one with all life. *[Name]* is gently but surely led into pathways of peace, of health, of happiness, and of success.

MEDITATIONS

My Meditation

My Creator's House

"You are always with me, and all that I have is yours."

Meditation is actually something that the mind does to itself. It is something of an awakening process, and in meditation and prayer we wish to arouse our imagination to the acceptance of the fact that God's house is right where we are, that we are really living in it now.

Today I am entering into my Creator's house. Today my Creator is coming out to meet me. Today I am going to make merry with all my siblings, with the whole world, because surely each person belongs to the heavenly realm and each is dear to the heart of God.

I know that in my Creator's house there is love, there is friendship, there is cooperation, there is peace. I know that in my Creator's house everyone is joyful, everyone is happy, everyone is contented. I know that in my Creator's house there is abundance for all. There is courage and hope and faith, there is laughter and song and dancing, and, brooding over the whole atmosphere of this household, quietness, peace and love penetrate every room.

I know that my Creator's table is spread with the gifts of life—everything that is necessary for my daily good. As I sit at the table of abundance which the law of good has provided for me, I do reverently give thanks for all that is mine, and I do earnestly desire that I may realize that this good is not mine alone, but mine to share with everyone I meet, mine to use and pass along, mine to multiply through faith.

MEDITATIONS

My Meditation

Toward Good

"Wherefore laying aside all malice, and all guile, and hypocrisies and envies, and all evil speakings, as newborn babes, desire the sincere milk of the word, that you may grow thereby."

I am turning from everything that denies the immediate presence of good. I am turning from everything that limits the power of God. I am turning from all doubt or fear, and, as a newborn baby, I am being fed from the substance of good and guided by the hand of love.

I have complete confidence in this guidance and perfect trust in the power that is guiding me. My whole mind is open, free, happy, buoyant. I enthusiastically expect an influx of power. I joyously receive the bounty, the manna from heaven, the good that God has provided. I gratefully accept the presence of a power greater than I am in everything I do.

I am to receive inspiration from on high. I am to have faith and acceptance. I am to listen deeply, and I am being guided. Therefore, I lay aside all doubt, all fear, all malice, all envy, all evil, and, as a newborn baby in the sincerity and simplicity of a child, I accept the realm of God here and now.

My Meditation

Complete Acceptance

In this meditation, we are going to see if we can draw very close to a spirit of acceptance. We wish to identify our lives with the divine presence and enter into conscious communion with the Spirit, which is within and around us.

"Let us not be weary in well doing: for in due season we shall reap, if we faint not." As you think about the meaning of these words and enter into the spirit of them, try to arrive at a place of complete acceptance in your mind, a place where you actually believe that there is a law of good and a power greater than you are responding to you. It is this inward feeling and acceptance that constitutes real faith, and it is a childlike attitude that helps you to surrender this faith into the law of good.

It was his complete surrender to the law of good that enabled

Jesus to perform wonderful miracles of faith. As you meditate, letting go of every disturbing thought, you turn quietly, peacefully, and reverently to the Spirit that is not only around you, but also within. It is this Spirit with which we commune and the law of good in which we have faith.

I know that I can make conscious use of the divine law of my being. I know that this law reacts immediately and creatively to my faith. I know that when I speak this word for myself, there is a direct reaction toward me. I know that when I speak it for others, there is a direct reaction toward them.

There is no doubt or uncertainty in my consciousness. I identify myself with the good I desire. I have complete confidence that the law of good will respond to me by creating the object of this desire. I have a quiet contentment and an inner sense of peace. I have an enthusiastic sense of well-being.

I know that all the power there is is for me; therefore, I put on the whole armor of faith. Today and every day, I expect good. I anticipate meeting new friends. I joyously anticipate contacting new situations that will increase my livingness. My life is an adventure. I know that wonderful things are going to happen to me. I know that everything I do will turn into good for myself and for others.

My Meditation

Spirit Hears

"I know that you hear me always."

Believing that the Spirit is right where I am, and that the law of God, which is a law of good, is active in my affairs now, I do sincerely and simply affirm that I am one with this good. I believe that this good includes everything right and necessary to my happiness, to my peace, to my mental and physical well-being. And I believe that this law of good brings success and happiness to myself and to others.

There is nothing to be afraid of. Joy goes before me and prepares the way. Love guides me to the fulfillment of everything that is good. Peace surrounds me. I rest in quiet contentment, knowing that all the power and all the presence that there is is behind every good purpose that I hold in mind.

It is my desire that I will bless everyone I contact, that I will bring hope and joy to every situation I meet. It is my desire that I will have sympathy and love for everyone I meet. It is my desire to help every person I contact. It is my desire that I will bless every situation I am in. Joyfully, I wait on the law of good. Gladly, I enter into communion with life, and with a deep sense of gratitude, I give thanks.

MEDITATIONS

My Meditation

Personal Peace

The purpose of affirmative prayer and meditation is to unite your mind with the divine presence, to identify yourself with This Thing Called Life, with the power greater than you are, and with the law of good. Take this thought into your meditation today: "And in whatsoever house you enter, first say 'peace be to this house'." Realize that the house you enter means everywhere you go and the occupants of this house represent everyone you meet.

Peace is the power in the heart of God. I recognize this peace in which I live as being closer to me than my very breath, nearer than my hands and feet. There is a calm and a peace at the center of my being and at the center of everyone's being. There is a confidence and a joy at the center of everything. It is this peace, this joy, and this confidence that I meet in every person and in every situation. I bring peace to everything I contact. I bring joy to everyone I meet. And my peace and joy makes their peace joyful.

There is a law of good governing my life that automatically draws me to people and circumstances that make life full, complete, and happy. This happiness I bring to others, and this same happiness I receive from them. It is my desire that everything I do, say, and think will bless everyone and everything I contact, and even as I desire this blessing for others, I receive it back into myself.

To the presence that knows all things and that can do all things, be glory and honor, dominion and power, both now and forever. Amen.

My Meditation

Found in God

"It is God who works in you."

Realize that you have an intimate relationship with This Thing Called Life, and above everything else, see if you can feel the immediate presence of this life.

I am now letting go of all fear and doubt. I am loosing it and letting it go as I affirm the presence of perfect life within me. I feel that I am entering into its harmony. I am one with its rhythm. I feel the rhythm and the pulsation of the universe flowing through me with perfect power.

I am entering into a deep conviction that all is well with myself and with everyone else. I am entering into conscious union with others, into harmony with everything that transpires in my everyday life, and into a deep sense of gratitude for life itself

As I let go of everything that denies the goodness of life, I feel that God is giving life back to me as it actually is—in love, in harmony, and in peace. I rejoice in this self-discovery, that I see myself not lost but found in God.

My Meditation

Lifted Up

"I will lift up my eyes unto the hills, from whence comes my help. My help comes from the Lord, who made heaven and earth."

I am lifting up my whole thought to the inflow of divine strength and wisdom, and I believe that today and tomorrow and every day I am in silent partnership with God, the living Spirit almighty.

I believe that the Spirit goes before me and prepares the way. I believe that every doorway is open, that new opportunities are presenting themselves. New ideas are coming into my mind. I am meeting new situations. My whole experience is increasing in love, in friendship and in activity. I expect to be successful. I anticipate being prosperous. I gladly share everything that I have with others, realizing that in this great game of life, I am not only one with God but one with all people.

Divine intelligence flows through me, causing me to think and act in such a way as to bring good into my experience and into the experience of everyone with whom I deal. My business is God's business, and God's business is my business. God's business is always successful, and I am in partnership with all the presence and all the power there is. I am one with the only mind there is. I am one with the infinite presence. I am one with the eternal good.

MEDITATIONS

My Meditation

Enthusiastic Living

"Let the peace of God rule in your hearts."

"The word of Christ dwells in you richly in all wisdom."

"Whatever you do, do it heartily as unto the Lord."

We all wish the peace of God to be in our hearts. We wish to so live that the words of Christ will dwell in our minds, and we all wish to live joyously so that whatever we do may be done heartily and with enthusiasm. In your meditation today, see if you can arrive at this enthusiastic way of living.

I am affirming today that the peace of God rules my heart and the word of Christ dwells in me in wisdom. I am affirming that divine wisdom governs my heart, causing me to live in love and in union with all people.

I am affirming that all the life, all the vitality, all the energy, and all the enthusiasm there is is flowing through me, flowing out into action in everything I do, say, and think. I am affirming that the whole world is governed by wisdom, that love rules the heart of humanity, guiding leaders everywhere into pathways of hope, of peace, and of prosperity.

I am affirming the divine presence in human events. I am affirming divine wisdom in human judgments. I am affirming divine love as the motivating power behind all human action. I am uniting my spiritual conviction with people of faith everywhere in the affirmation that the peace of God does rule our hearts, that the word of Christ does swell richly in us, in all wisdom.

My Meditation

Prayer of Love and Friendship

"That they may be one, even as we are one."

I perceive the Spirit of wholeness, the union of all life. Deep within my being, I know that I am one with all people, all ages, all events. I am one with the infinite and the eternal. I am one with all the goodness there is, one with all power, and one with the only presence—the presence of God in me. In everyone I meet, I perceive this union. I meet it with joy. I am accepted by it, even as I accept it. I cannot reject myself, nor can I be rejected by myself. There is only one self, which is God, the eternal self. I am one with this self, one with love, one with joy, one with friendship.

This oneness peoples my world with the loving attention of innumerable friends, with every human manifestation of the divine reality. I appreciate this friend of mine, whom I meet in innumerable forms. Everywhere I go, I will meet God. Everywhere I look, I will see God. I am held in the embrace of the eternal presence. Every thought of disunion, separation, or unhappiness is forever gone from my mind. Love, joy, and companionship are permanently established in my experience.

My Meditation

Prayer of the Perfect Heart

I am a center of divine perfection within me. I am free from every sense of burden, strain, or tension. My pulsation is in harmony with the infinite rhythm of the universe. There is no burden, no strain. I am not troubled or concerned over the future, nor worried over the past, nor afraid of the present. Perfect love casts out all fear. The rhythm of my action is in perfect relaxation. Its vitality is complete. The walls of my being are whole.

Joyfully, the Spirit circulates through me, reaching every atom of my being with the message of perfect life and happiness. All tension, fear, and strain is removed. I rest in calm assurance that eternal goodness is forever

around me. I am free from all condemnation, judgment, or bondage. My whole life is joy, fulfillment, the
happiness of expression, and complete freedom. There
is one heart. That is the heart of pure Spirit. That is my
heart. That is the center of my being. I sing the song of
the perfect heart.

My Meditation

Prayer of Perfect Health

This prayer is a recognition of the divine indwelling Spirit.

The Spirit within me is circulating through every atom of my being, flowing in joy, carrying the life-giving essence of love and wisdom, truth and beauty, surging through every atom of my being with divine power, energy, and perfection. Infinite Spirit of wholeness and happiness within me, joyful is its flow, complete is its surge, perfect is its circulation. Every idea that enters my consciousness, everything that enters my physical being, is assimilated in the flow of this divine life, harmonized through its unity, and directed by its intelligence. Everything is assimilated and digested.

Therefore, the activity and thought of my being are balanced and perfect. Every function and organ is in harmony with the rhythmic flow of the universe. Nothing remains in me but the truth. Truth eliminates everything unlike itself. There is nothing unlike truth. There is no stagnation, no inaction and no wrong action. There is one actor, acting in and through me, one wholeness manifest in every part of my being.

I rejoice in this circulation and flow of Spirit. The peace and calm of eternal well-being—the joyful recognition of my union with good, the glad opening up of the gates of my whole being, that I may become saturated with the essence of perfection—is now complete.

MEDITATIONS

My Meditation

Prayer for a Successful Business

Let us assume that our business has become sluggish or inactive. We then turn to the all-pervading presence for its inspiration and guidance in the same manner that we pray for a physical healing, knowing that our success in business, the activity that we generate through the operation of the law, depends on our ability to conceive. We therefore eliminate from our thinking thoughts of failure, limitation, or poverty.

No matter what others may say, think, or do, I know that I am a success now. I radiate joy and am filled with faith, hope, and expectancy. I refuse to think of failure or to doubt my own power, because I am depending on the principle of life itself for all that I will ever need.

I know that there comes to my attention everything that I need in order to project my business in every direction with the certainty of success. I see this expansion and pray that it may bless everyone who contacts it, that I may serve all who come near me, that all who know me will feel my love and friendship and will sense a warmth and color within me.

I pray that everyone who touches my business in any way will be uplifted and satisfied. I bless and praise everyone who is in any way connected with my business. I draw them to me with the irresistible charm of divine union. I serve them and am served by them. The reciprocal action of love prospers those I serve, as well as me. I am success, happiness, and fulfillment.

My Meditation

Group Prayer

The one supreme Spirit is within, around, and through every member of this group. Each person is a center of God-conscious life, truth, and action.

Infinite intelligence governs, sustains, and animates every member of this body. Good alone goes from them, and good alone returns to them. Infinite Mind establishes harmony and right adjustment of all personal, family, business, and social affairs or conditions in the life of each member. Each is supplied with every good thing. Each is happy, radiant, and complete. The Spirit of God manifests in each one as peace, harmony, and wholeness.

Everything that anyone of this group does, says, or thinks is governed by infinite intelligence and inspired by divine wisdom. Each is guided by divine intelligence into right action. Each is surrounded by friendship, love, and beauty.

Each person is the manifestation of the divine Spirit that never tires, that is birthless, deathless, and limitless. Each is receptive to the inexhaustible energy of the universe and to divine guidance. Each person in this group is conscious of complete happiness, abundant health, and increasing prosperity. Each is aware of their partnership with the Infinite. Each knows that everything they do will prosper. Each is conscious of inner peace and poise. Each immediately becomes conscious of a more abundant life.

My Meditation

A Prayer for World Peace

"The earth is the Lord's and the fullness thereof."

I know there is only one mind, which is the mind of God, in which all people live and move and have their being.

I know there is a divine pattern for humanity, and within this pattern there is infinite harmony and peace, cooperation, unity, and mutual helpfulness.

I know that the mind of humankind, being one with the mind of God, will discover the method, the way, and the means best fitted to permit the flow of divine love between individuals and nations. Thus, harmony, peace, cooperation, unity, and mutual helpfulness will be experienced by all.

I know there will be a free interchange of ideas, cultures, spiritual concepts, ethics, educational systems, and scientific discoveries, because all good belongs to all alike.

I know that because the divine mind has created us all, we are bound together in one infinite and perfect unity.

In bringing about world peace, I know that all people and all nations will remain individual but unified for the common purpose of promoting peace, happiness, harmony, and prosperity.

I know that deep within every person, the divine pattern of perfect peace is already implanted.

I now declare that in each person and in leaders of thought everywhere, this divine pattern moves into action and form, to the end that all nations and all people will live together in peace, harmony, and prosperity forever.

So it is, *now.*

My Meditation

Meditation for Right Thinking

I believe in the power greater than I am. I believe in the divine presence in which I live and move and have my being. I am thinking back to the center of my being, where this presence exists in all its beauty and all its peace.

I know that divine intelligence helps me to control my thinking and causes me to live with joy and in calm expectancy of good. I am permitting myself to be guided by this intelligence. As I wait on it and let it flow through me and out into action, I know that I will be guided in everything I do. I know I will bless everyone I meet. I will bring new life to every situation I contact.

My whole mind and thought respond to this with complete conviction, and I feel today and every day that the power of the living spirit flows through me and makes perfect the way before me, radiating joy and love to everyone and to everything.

My Meditation

Meditation for Abundance

Believing that God is the invisible partner in my life, I now affirm that divine love goes before me and prepares the way. I permit myself to be guided. There is something deep within me that knows exactly what I ought to do and how I ought to do it. I am listening to this divine presence and permitting it to direct my path. I not only believe that it can, but I know that it will. Thoughts and ideas will come to me, and I will be led to follow them out in my everyday life. I will be impelled into right action.

I know how to meet every situation in calm trust and with the complete conviction that divine intelligence is guiding me. I wish to do only that which is constructive and life-giving. Therefore, I know that everything I do is prospered. Everything I touch will be quickened into a newness of life and action. Every constructive purpose in my life will be fulfilled.

I thank God for this increase that is mine. I accept divine guidance. I believe that I am in silent partnership with all the power all the presence and all the love there is. I place my life entirely and completely under the protection and guidance of this power, and I rest in complete faith that everything I do is prospered.

My Meditation

Meditation for Love

*"If we love one another, God dwells in us
and God's love is perfected in us."*

I believe that God is love. I believe that love is at the center of everything. Therefore, I accept love as the healing power of life. I permit love to reach out from me to every person I meet. I believe that love is returned to me from every person I meet.

I trust the guidance of love because I believe it is the power of good in the universe. I feel that love is flowing through me to heal every situation I meet, to help every person I contact. Love opens the way before me and makes it perfect, straight, and immediate.

Love forgives everything unlike itself. It purifies everything. Love converts everything that seems commonplace into that which is wonderful. Love converts weakness into strength, fear into faith. Love is the all-conquering power of Spirit. As a small child walks in confidence with its parent, so I walk in confidence with life. As a child, through love, trusts its parent, so I put my whole trust in the love that I feel to be everywhere present, within, around, and through me, within, around, and through all people.

My Meditation

Freedom from Fear and Anxiety

*"Fear not, little flock, it is your
Creator's good pleasure to give you the realm."*

I am now letting go of every anxious thought. I am now surrendering any doubt or fear into the great heart of love. I am looking out on the world and saying, "This is my world because it is God's world." I am now thinking of all people: "These are my friends because they live and move and have their being in the Creator of us all." I am now receiving confidence and inspiration from the source of all life.

I believe that love is guiding me. I believe that there is a divine power that goes before me and makes perfect my way in joy and happiness. I believe this power is flowing through me to the joy and happiness of those around me. I have a faith, a conviction, an assurance at the center of my being. I have a love that envelops everything I contact and every person I meet. I have a friend within me who knows all my needs.

I accept the realm that God has given. I accept the life that God has implanted in me, and this life reaches out to everything around me, in joy and gladness and with the blessed assurance that all is well.

My Meditation

Meditation for Faith

"I will lead them in paths that they have not known."

I am bringing all my problems to the altar of faith, and I know that every true desire of my heart will be fulfilled through the power of love. My first desire is that all my thoughts and all my acts will give joy and gladness to everyone around me. I wish the healing power of love to flow through me to everyone.

I now believe that divine intelligence, which is the mind of God, is guiding, guarding, and directing my thoughts and acts.

I believe that God already knows the answer to this problem; therefore, I am letting go of the problem and I am listening to the answer as though it were sure. The answer to this problem not only exists in the mind of God, but I affirm that it is in my mind now, that something in me does know what to do.

I confidently wait on divine good. I expect to be guided. I joyfully accept this guidance with deep gratitude and with a great feeling of love and closeness to the divine presence that I know fills all space. I am open to new ideas, to new thoughts, new hopes and aspirations. This which so recently seemed a problem no longer exists, because the mind of God, which knows the answer, is quietly flowing through my thought and feeling. A great peace and joy come over me as I accept this answer from the giver of all life.

My Meditation

Meditation for Physical Health

"The spirit of God has made me,
and the breath of the Almighty has given me life."

My body is the temple of the living God, and I believe in the ability and the willingness of Spirit to sustain its own creation. I believe that every organ and function of my physical body is animated by the living Spirit within me. I have complete confidence in this Spirit. I know that I am loved of this Spirit and needed by it. I feel at home with it.

There is no condemnation, no judgment, and no fear in me. I feel that I belong to the world in which I live, that I love people and am loved of them. I have a deep sense of confidence and trust. I feel that I am secure in life and that I need no longer be anxious about anything. I am laying all of my fears and doubts aside and entering into quiet communion with the Spirit of confidence, of faith, and of acceptance.

I feel that my whole being is renewed, invigorated, and made alive. There is complete stillness and perfect peace at the center of my being as I wait on the presence that makes all things perfect.

My Meditation

Mirror of Life

"But we all, with open face beholding as in a glass the glory of the Lord, are changed into the same image from glory to glory, even as by the Spirit of the Lord."

With this meditation, look into the mirror of your life and see reflected there the beauty, the peace, the harmony, the love, and the prosperity you so sincerely desire, that the meaning of the above passage from Corinthians may come true, that you also may be changed from glory to glory by the Spirit of the Lord.

As I look out into the world, I see that there is nothing to fear. As I look back into my own mind, I know there is nothing in me that is afraid. My whole thought and atmosphere is filled with confidence, with hope, with trust, and with the acceptance of good. I expect the mirror of my experience to be filled with joy, and as I turn the magic lantern of my mind into the great mind and Spirit of the universe in which all things exist, I know that I am one with all peace, all power, and all good.

I am one with people and events. I meet everything with a sense of unity. I feel myself to be accepted by life. There is nothing in me that criticizes or harshly judges. There is nothing in me that receives condemnation.

I affirm the presence of good in everything I do and the guidance of love everywhere I go. I affirm that strength, enthusiasm, and vitality forever flow through me from the all-sustaining life of the universe. I affirm my union with God, and I know that there is nothing in the entire universe to be afraid of, nothing to avoid, nothing to run away from. I am at home in the universe wherever I may be—one with God, one with people, one with the perfect and abiding faith that knows no fear.

My Meditation

Certainty

"Commit your works unto the Lord,
and your purposes shall be established."

Believing that the Spirit of God is within and around me, and realizing that there is a real spiritual person within me who is one with God, I do commit all of my thoughts and acts into the keeping of a power greater than I am.

I open my consciousness to the influx of new ideas. I am not only asking for divine guidance, I am equally receiving it. I am not only recognizing God as the only power and presence and person there is in the universe, I am equally aware that God is recognizing me as the divine person God intended me to be.

Today and every day, I am led to think the right thoughts and I am impelled to act on them.

All sense of fear and doubt, of confusion or uncertainty, leaves me, and I feel the calm assurance that there is a presence that evermore enfolds me in its loving embrace.

I feel the certainty of faith, and this certainty I carry out into action in everything I do, say, and think. I am no longer alone or afraid. I am one with God and one with people and one with events. I am one with the activity of life and one with the beauty of wholeness.

My Meditation

As You Believe

"It is done unto you as you believe."

Believing that the final power of the universe is good, and accepting the simple thought that God is right where I am, I empty my mind of all confusion, I let go of every doubt and fear, and I turn away from every sense of want or lack or limitation as I lift up my thought to the great giver of all life with complete acceptance.

I now affirm that all the power there is and all the love there is and all the life there is belongs to me, as it does to everyone else. I let this power flow through me. I realize that this life is my life now. I believe that divine intelligence is always acting on my mind, telling me what is best to do, counseling me wisely and guiding me gently but surely into pathways of peace, of prosperity and happiness, into pathways of physical health and wholeness and into pathways that lead to loving companionship and right relations with others.

Knowing that we all live and move and have our being in God, I find myself at one with all people. Realizing that love is the great motivating power of life, I permit this love to flow through me to others. Accepting that my faith is operated on by a power greater than I am, I persistently hold this thought in mind, that my faith, my conviction, my sense of the divine presence will operate on everything I touch and everyone I meet, to help, to heal, to prosper, and to bless.

My Meditation

God Is Here

As we join in uniting our faith in this great search for God, actually believe that you are finding God here and now.

Believing that God is in and through everything, and believing that God can be revealed through me to everyone, I sincerely seek to so live, to so think, and to so act that kindness, joy, love, and faith will flow from me to everyone and everything I contact.

I am glorifying the God in me by recognizing the God in others and seeking to live in union with the eternal good that flows through all.

Believing that there is one life animating everything and one power sustaining everything and one intelligence governing everything, I surrender my intellect and my will to this divine influence, knowing that only good can come from the source of all being.

I surrender all littleness, all fear, all doubt, to its certainty. I surrender all weakness to its strength, all sadness to its joy, all failure to its completion. I surrender earth to heaven. I surrender death into life. And I know that I am in the keeping of good forevermore.

My Meditation

Better Understanding

"We are a colony of heaven, and we wait for Christ, who will transform the body that belongs to our low estate until it resembles the body of glory."

Today, seek to better understand and inwardly feel the meaning of the divine body that is perfect. Be certain to identify this physical body of yours with the Spirit within you, which is already complete and perfect.

I am one with the infinite Spirit of wholeness. The Creator and I are one. This infinite, indwelling glory now manifests itself in and through every cell of my being.

This body of mine is a temple of the living God. As I wait on this living God, I know that every action, every cell, every atom of my being is at this instant brought into perfect harmony and perfect health, that every shadow of doubt or worry or fear is instantly dispelled from the radiance of God's glory, which is within.

I am quickened with the life of God. I am blessed in the love of God. I am secure in God's divine keeping.

I do decree that the whole body of humanity—the whole human race—at this very moment, expresses and reflects the nature of God, bringing peace, health, love, and unity to everyone on earth.

My Meditation

Ageless Spirit

"You will show me the path of life: in your presence is fullness of joy: at the right hand there are pleasures forever more."

As you dwell on the meaning of these words quietly in your own mind, see if you cannot come into a complete realization that you are one with the ageless Spirit.

In the quiet of my mind, I realize that I am one with the eternal newness of life. The Spirit is creating in and through me now. My body is alive with the life of God. My body is illumined by the light of God. There is no darkness of discouragement, despair, or defeat. My mind is refreshed in the one Mind that eternally gives of itself to its creation.

All that the Creator has is mine. I open my heart to accept the good gifts of joy and happiness, of enthusiasm. I open my heart to know that the ageless Spirit is my life.

I decree that my body and my experiences will reflect the image of life in all its newness, and I will dance and sing through the days of my years with gladness in my mind. I will dwell in the house of the Lord forever, knowing that my cup is full to overflowing with the only life there is—the life and the eternal youth of God.

My Meditation

Open Heart

"Let not your heart be troubled, neither let it be afraid."

Find the assurance that comes from conscious communion with the Spirit in which you live and move and have your being.

I am now established in the presence of infinite good. The life of God is my life right now. The mind of God is my mind right now.

I open my heart to the influx of Spirit and know that the love that floods my being heals my body and dispels every shadow of doubt and fear and anxiety.

The truth of my spiritual being sets me free from the bondage of ignorance. Divine intelligence directs my thoughts and my path, so that I may move into life's activities with a calm and poise and assurance that never wavers.

I dwell in the house of the Lord forever and rejoice in the divine companionship of the infinite presence that sustains me in all that I do. All that the Creator has is mine. This I accept. This I express.

My Meditation

Preparing the Mind

"Let us, then, prepare our minds to give birth to a future bright with hope and constant fulfillment."

There is a very definite way of meditation. We call this "using the power greater than we are," which is This Thing Called Life. We are surrounded by a universal law of good that acts on our thinking.

"If anyone be in Christ, they are a new creature: old things are passed away; behold, all things are made new."

As you turn to the presence that is the divine parent of all of us, realize that you are uniting your thought with the creative power that is behind all things. As you think of this divine creative power as your parent that is in heaven, think of this presence as being within you as well as around you.

I know that I am one with this divine presence, and I know that I am one with the law of good. I am making my mind open and receptive to the divine Spirit, to its presence and its guidance. I am opening my mind to the influx of divine ideas.

There is something within me that receives these ideas and acts on them intelligently. I am led and guided and directed in everything I do. I am inspired to think new thoughts, to receive new ideas, and to enter into a larger experience. I expect all this to happen. I permit it to happen.

Realizing that I am rooted in pure Spirit, from which I draw my life, I know that there is a perfect pattern of my physical body in this divine Spirit, and I know that every function and every action of my physical body is animated by this divine pattern, sustained by it, kept in continual health and well-being.

Knowing that God, the one eternal parent of us all, is in everyone, I recognize this Spirit in everyone I meet. Therefore, I am one with all people and all people are one with me. Recognizing this same presence in all nature, I feel myself to be one with God's world and one with all God's people, because God is over all, through all, and in all.

My Meditation

Peace and Good

"Acquaint now yourself with God, and be at peace; thereby good shall come unto you."

To acquaint yourself with God means to feel the divine presence within and around you. To be at peace means to relax and let the Divine flow through you.

I am at peace because I know that I live and move and have my being in the divine Spirit that flows through everything. I feel this perfect presence at the center of my own being, and I feel that divine guidance is governing all my affairs.

I do let go and let God. As a child relaxes in the arms of its parent, so I relax in the thought of the all-sustaining good, the ever-present love, and the all-knowing wisdom.

Tonight, as I seek the repose of peace, I will say to myself, "I sleep in peace and wake in joy and live in a consciousness of good." And my first thought in the morning will be, "Today I am sustained. Today I am guided. Today I am led. Today I give the world the best I have. Today the God in me meets the God in others and in events. Today is God's day, and it is a good day. God goes with me. Love sustains me. Goodness directs me. And all the power that there is envelops me in its perfect presence."

I am one in God. Right now, I am at peace.

MEDITATIONS

My Meditation

Words of Power and Life

It is wonderful that we are free to choose words of power and words of life. This itself is the gift of God—a gift so freely given but so seldom used. We wish to use this power so that we may get more out of life and contribute more to it. Begin this moment.

There is a spiritual command to which I listen and to which I will respond. From this moment, I will let the words of love and life and peace speak clearly and with authority in all my experience. No matter what happens around me, no matter what happens in the world, I know that This Thing Called Life is forever proclaiming its own wholeness. It is saying to me, "Life" and "Love" and "Peace."

I will listen to this still, small voice as it speaks within, and I will proclaim its words of peace and life and love so that they become life and power to me. And because they become life and power to me, they will bless those around me. They will bring happiness and confidence and joy and health to those to whom I speak my healing words. Just as the Creator has given to me of God's life, so I may give life to the world in which I live, to become a message of faith and hope and love.

My Meditation

Free from Anxiety

"Fear not, because it is your Creator's good pleasure to give you the realm."

Affirmative prayer is a direct line of communion with God. Affirmative prayer means that we clear our minds of doubt and fear, and turn in faith to the great giver of life. It means that we become aware of the presence of God within and around us, here and now. It means that we affirm this presence and accept it, quietly, confidently, and peacefully.

I am now letting go of every anxious thought. I am now surrendering any doubt or fear into the great heart of love. I am looking out on the world and saying, "This is my world because it is God's world." I am now thinking of all people. These are my friends, because they live and move and have their being in the Creator of us all. I am now receiving confidence and inspiration from the source of all life.

I believe that love is guiding me. I believe that there is a divine power that goes before me and makes perfect my way in joy and happiness. I believe that this power is flowing through me to the joy and happiness of those around me. I have a faith, a conviction, an assurance at the center of my being. I have a love that envelops everything I contact and every person I meet. I have a friend within me who knows all my needs.

I accept the realm that God has given. I accept the life that God has implanted in me, and this life reaches out to everything around me, in joy and gladness and with the blessed assurance that all is well.

My Meditation

Overcome Evil with Good

*Evil is the negation of good and will dissipate itself just as dark-
ness is dissipated when we introduce a light. This is why Jesus
told us to resist not evil, and St. Paul told us to think on whatsoever things are good and lovely. This is the meaning of your
meditation today, your prayer of affirmation, that you affirm the
presence of good and, in so doing, permit the law of right action
to make each today and each tomorrow a more complete fulfillment of all the divine promises.*

*Affirmative prayer accepts the answer even before it knows
how it is to be brought about. This is the highest act of faith we
can assume toward this thing called life and the God who gave
it. Enter into your meditation in complete acceptance that good
is the final and absolute power in the universe, and as you commune with your own soul, directly and personally, and with the
divine Spirit that flows through you, do it reverently, simply,
but with complete conviction.*

I turn the searchlight of truth on every apparent evil in my experience. This light dissolves every image of evil. The manifestation of good is complete. My every thought and act is an expression of the goodness that flows from life. The Divine circulates through me automatically, freely. Every atom of my being is animated by its action.

Today I recognize the abundance of life. I animate everything in my experience with this idea. I remember only the good. I accept only the good. I expect only the good. This is all that I experience.

I know that my word penetrates any unbelief in my mind, casts out fear, removes doubts, clears away obstacles, permitting that which is enduring, perfect, and true to be realized. I have complete faith and acceptance that all the statements I make will be carried out as I have believed. I relax and let a power greater than I am work for me, in me, and through me.

I know that there is a presence and a perfect law irresistibly drawing into my experience everything that makes life happy and worthwhile. Whatever belongs to me will come to me. I am compelled to recognize my good, to understand and accept it and to act on it. With joy, I enter into the fulfillment of life, and I know that it is good.

My Meditation

Gift of Heaven

Today I am receiving the gifts of heaven. Today I know that even as I ask, I will receive. I meet life in joy and gladness. I expect to be guided and intelligently directed in everything I do. I expect to meet good and love and friendship everywhere I go.

Even as I expect to receive, so I desire to give. It is my sincere desire that everyone I meet will be blessed, that everything I touch will be made whole. It is my desire that joy will flow from me in peace and happiness, bringing a sense of well-being and comfort and assurance to those around me.

Lifting up my own thought to the secret place of the most high within me, I feel that I do receive a benediction from heaven and, with it, the gifts of life, which I freely distribute. I know that as I gladly give of myself to others, so will something from them come back to me, to go out again, blessing and healing.

May the presence of the great and divine giver become real to me, and may the gifts of heaven be received by me, and may the good that I possess be shared with others.

My Meditation

Golden Key

"He is not here; but is risen."

There is a golden key to life. This key is in your own hand now, placed there by the Infinite. It is up to you to turn this key in the lock of your individual experience, to open the door of your experience to a larger hope and the greater possibility. It is the privilege of all of us to enter into a realization of the resurrection today, to join that triumphant procession of the ever-expanding soul. Let us realize that the resurrection is a symbol of the resurrection of all. Listen quietly, peacefully, and confidently as you commune with that Spirit who is not a God of the dead, but of the living.

God is life, and in God there is no death. God is love, and perfect love casts out all fear. As I enter into this life and this love and commune with this divine presence, I know that I am one with the living Spirit forever. I know that love guides me now and always, as it must all people. I enter into my divine inheritance today. I know that in my Creator's house are many mansions. Today is God's day, and tomorrow will be God's day, and so will all the tomorrows that will ever transpire.

Love prepares the way for me here, and love prepares the way for me there. I sing the song of eternity. I chant the hymn of the living. God is not dead; God is risen.

As I think of my loved ones who have entered the larger life, I know that they are not dead; they are just away. I know that they walk in the garden of God and waft back to me a kiss from the realm of heaven.

My Meditation

Meditation

I Believe

I believe in God, the living Spirit Almighty—one indestructible, absolute and self-existent cause. This One manifests itself in and through all creation but is not absorbed by its creation. The manifest universe is the body of God. It is the logical and necessary outcome of the infinite self-knowingness of God.

I believe in the incarnation of the Spirit in everyone and that all people are incarnations of the one Spirit.

I believe in the eternality, the immortality, and the continuity of the individual soul, forever and ever expanding.

I believe that heaven is within me and that I experience it to the degree that I become conscious of it.

I believe the ultimate goal of life to be a complete emancipation from all discord of every nature, and that this goal is sure to be attained by all.

I believe in the unity of all life, and that the highest God and the innermost God are one God.

I believe that God is personal to all who feel this indwelling presence.

I believe in the direct revelation of truth through the intuitive and spiritual nature of the individual, and that any person may become a revealer of truth who lives in close contact with the indwelling God.

I believe that the universal Spirit, which is God, operates through a universal Mind, which is the law of God; and that we are surrounded by this creative Mind, which receives the direct impress of our thought and acts on it.

I believe in the healing of the sick through the power of this Mind.

I believe in the control of conditions through the power of this Mind.

I believe in the eternal goodness, the eternal loving-kindness, and the eternal givingness of life to all.

I believe in my own soul, my own spirit, and my own destiny, because I understand that the life of all is God.

My Meditation

ERNEST SHURTLEFF HOLMES (1887–1960), an ordained Divine Science minister, was founder of a spiritual movement known as Religious Science, a part of the New Thought movement, whose spiritual philosophy is known as Science of Mind. He was the author of *The Science of Mind* and numerous other metaphysical books, as well as founder of *Science of Mind* magazine, in continuous publication since 1927.

NEWT LIST is the foremost publisher of updated editions of spiritual classic texts. Newt List titles are edited to provide contemporary language structure and idioms that have evolved since the original manuscript was published. We revise punctuation and capitalizations, and adjust sentence structure when appropriate, as well as update certain words or terms that have since become obscure, as long as those changes do not affect the author's intention or meaning. More valuable for readers today, though, is Newt List's procedure of changing of gender forms. In the time of original publication, these classic books generally used masculine forms when referring to God or humankind. Newt List updates all its books using gender-neutral language, making the ideas in them apply more broadly to all readers.

For more books by Ernest Holmes
and other New Thought authors,
visit NewtList.com.

Made in the USA
Las Vegas, NV
27 January 2021